Shakespeare for Students, Second Edition, Volume 3

Project Editor
Anne Marie Hacht

Rights Acquisition and Management
Lisa Kincade, Robbie McCord, Lista Person, Kelly Quin, and Andrew Specht

Manufacturing
Rita Wimberley

Imaging
Lezlie Light

Product Design
Pamela A. E. Galbreath and Jennifer Wahi

Vendor Administration
Civie Green

Product Manager
Meggin Condino

LIBRARY OF CONGRESS CATALOGING-IN-PUBLICATION DATA

Shakespeare for students: critical interpretations of Shakespeare's plays and poetry.-2nd ed. / Anne Marie Hacht, editor; foreword by Cynthia Burnstein.

p. cm.

Includes bibliographical references and index.

ISBN-13: 978-1-4144-1255-9 (set)
ISBN-10: 1-4144-1255-X (set)
ISBN-13: 978-1-4144-1256-6 (v. 1)
ISBN-10: 1-4144-1256-8 (v. 1)
[etc.]

1. Shakespeare, William, 1564–1616—Outlines, syllabi, *etc.* 2. Shakespeare, William, 1564–1616—Criticism and interpretation. 3. Shakespeare, William, 1564–1616—Examinations-Study guides. I. Hacht, Anne Marie.

PR2987.S47 2007

822.3'3—dc22 2007008901

ISBN-13
978-1-4144-1255-9 (set)
978-1-4144-1256-6 (vol. 1)
978-1-4144-1258-0 (vol. 2)
978-1-4144-1259-7 (vol. 3)

ISBN-10
1-1444-1255-X (set)
1-4144-1256-8 (vol. 1)
1-4144-1258-4 (vol. 2)
1-4144-1259-2 (vol. 3)

This title is also available as an e-book.
ISBN-13 978-1-4144-2937-3 (set) ISBN-10 1-4144-2937-1 (set)
Contact your Gale, an imprint of Cengage Learning sales representative for ordering information.

Printed in the United States of America

10 9 8 7 6 5 4 3 2 1

Richard III

William Shakespeare

1592

Introduction

Although *Richard III* was first published in 1597, most scholars believe that this play about the rise and fall of a wicked king was written several years earlier, probably in 1592 or 1593, and was first performed shortly afterward. Evidence shows that it was popular from the beginning. The Elizabethan actor Richard Burbage achieved distinction playing Richard III, and the character's final line—"A horse! A horse! My kingdom for a horse!"—was already famous by the time Richard Corbet wrote a poem about the play in 1618 or 1621. Historians believe that Shakespeare's audiences would have especially appreciated the patriotic speech given by Richmond, who becomes King Henry VII in the last act and was Queen Elizabeth I's grandfather.

Early critical assessment of *Richard III* was mixed. Sir William Cornwallis (1600) and William Winstanley (1660), for example, objected to Shakespeare's portrayal of King Richard as "a monster." In contrast, the poet John Milton (1650) argued that the character in the play was "true to his historical counterpart." Today, most scholars agree that Shakespeare based the drama primarily on Edward Hall's *The Union of the Two Noble and Illustre Famelies of Lancastre and Yorke* (1548). Hall's work relies on both fact and fiction to tell the history of King Richard III's family, the House of York, and its long power struggle—known as the Wars of the Roses—with King Henry VII's family, the House of Lancaster. A secondary source was probably Raphael Holinshed's *Chronicles of England, Scotland, and Ireland* (1587). In turn, each of these works was based upon Sir Thomas More's witty and ironic *Historie of King Richard the Thirde*, published around 1513. In this account, More—who grew up in the household of the bishop of Ely, a minister to Henry VII—used a dry, almost humorous tone to describe Richard as hunchbacked, tyrannical, and evil.

Shakespeare's play varies from its sources in numerous ways but two are of particular importance. The first is that, although Shakespeare borrowed More's ironic narrative tone, he placed it in Richard's mouth, so that the character becomes a complex, semicomical villain who laughs at himself and others even while he is plotting to do harm. The fact that *Richard III* functions as a sequel to Shakespeare's three plays on the previous monarch, King Henry VI, accounts for the second of Shakespeare's significant modifications: in *Richard III*, Margaret, the widow of Henry VI—the Lancastrian king who was murdered by Richard in *Henry VI, Part Three*—remains in England, where the play is set, rather than sailing home to France, as she did according to history. Onstage, Margaret voices her opinion on the action in the play, predicting the doom and misery that will serve as her revenge on Richard and his supporters. In cursing those who brought about her and her husband's downfall, Margaret serves the same dramatic function as a chorus; a chorus, or individual choral figures, are sometimes used to describe events that occur before the beginning of a play or to comment on the play's action as it unfolds.

Richard's complexity and Margaret's haunting presence have generated much critical discussion, especially with regard to the play's themes of divine retribution. Richard's coronation comes toward the end of the Wars of the Roses, a long period of bloody civil strife, and some critics argue that his wickedness functions as both divine punishment against the warring parties and also as a method of cleansing England in preparation for a new era of peace. Margaret proves intricately involved in the development of the play, with her curses on each guilty character eventually being fulfilled. Above all, Richard is the central focus of the play. He is a ruthless, compellingly witty character who arguably has firm control of the people and events around him. In large measure thanks to Richard's dazzling wickedness, *Richard III* remains one of Shakespeare's most popular plays.

Plot Summary

Act 1, Scene 1

At the beginning of *Richard III*, on a London street, Richard, Duke of Gloucester and brother to King Edward IV, remarks that times of war have come and gone—and since his deformed person (he was purportedly hunchbacked) turns him away from romantic or peaceful interests, he will play the villain and convince King Edward that their other brother, George, Duke of Clarence, is a threat. Indeed, Clarence enters, guarded by Brakenbury, and laments that he is being imprisoned simply for bearing a name that starts with the letter *G*; a wizard has told King Edward that someone named so should be disinherited. Feigning sympathy, Richard declares that Queen Elizabeth and her brother Earl Rivers must have slandered him. Brakenbury interrupts, and as Clarence is led away, Richard promises aid to his brother. Once alone, Richard remarks that he intends to have Clarence murdered immediately. Lord Hastings, himself just released from prison, arrives to note that King Edward is sick. When Hastings leaves, Richard declares that he intends to marry Lady Anne, whose father-in-law and husband—King Henry VI and his son Edward —Richard recently killed.

Act 1, Scene 2

Lady Anne is seeing the coffin of Henry VI transported through the streets, and the funeral procession pauses so that she can mourn his death—and curse his murderer, Richard. As they prepare to move on, Richard enters and forces them to pause again. When Anne curses Richard to his face, he begs for pity and flatters her. He also denies having killed her husband, blaming Edward instead, but admits to killing Henry, who he claims is better off in heaven. He then professes a desire to gain Lady Anne's bedchamber, asserting that he in fact killed both men because he was moved by her beauty. She still wishes revenge on Richard, who says that he will love Anne better than did her deceased husband. He then expounds upon how he had never been moved to shed a tear until he was struck by her beauty. When she continues to scorn him, he offers his sword, that she might slay him. She moves to do so—but when he again praises her beauty, she lowers the weapon. He then tells her that if she again asks him to kill himself, he would; she does not, however, and when Richard offers her his ring, she accepts it.

Richard then bids Anne retire to Crosby House, where he will meet her after directing Henry VI's body to its burial place. When left alone, he reveals that he does not intend to "keep" Anne for long. He even professes amazement that Anne should show him any favor, given how virtuous her deceased husband had been. In the meantime, he will attire himself well.

Act 1, Scene 3

At the palace, Queen Elizabeth is consoled by her brother and sons about the possible death of her husband; Queen Elizabeth also laments that her own son Edward, the heir apparent, would be placed under the guardianship of Richard if King Edward dies. The Duke of Buckingham and Lord Stanley then arrive to note that the king is in fair health and wishes to make peace between parties that have been quarreling recently.

Richard then enters to complain that people such as Lord Grey have been unfairly speaking ill of him; Queen Elizabeth retorts that Richard is simply jealous of the political advancement of her kin. Richard accuses Queen Elizabeth of causing Clarence's imprisonment, which she denies. Queen Margaret, the widow of King Henry VI, then enters to watch the quarreling unnoticed. While Richard speaks of the good deeds he has done on behalf of King Edward, Margaret criticizes him bitterly in asides. Richard accuses Rivers and the others of backing Henry's house of Lancaster, to which Rivers replies that he was simply serving his king.

At length, Margaret comes forth to declare that she is ignoring her banishment and demanding recognition of the extreme sorrows she has suffered. Invoking the earlier death of Rutland, Richard rouses Queen Elizabeth and the others present to condemn Margaret. Furious, Margaret curses nearly everyone present for their treachery to her family; she lays her longest curse on Richard, warning the others that they will one day wish they had supported that cursing. She expresses no ill will toward Buckingham alone, who tries to make peace, but Margaret insists that God will see that her revenge is had and that they will all regret allying with Richard. When Margaret leaves, Richard plays the role of a penitent and forgiving Christian.

After Catesby arrives and ushers everyone else off toward King Edward, Richard muses over how he has convinced Derby, Hastings, and Buckingham that Queen Elizabeth and her relatives conspired against Clarence. The two men whom Richard has hired to kill Clarence then arrive and accept a warrant from Richard. He urges them to kill Clarence without listening to any of his pleas.

Act 1, Scene 4

Clarence relates to the Keeper the dream he had the previous night, in which Richard seemed to knock him overboard accidentally as they were crossing the sea to France; after long drowning and gazing at the morbid wonders beneath the sea, he traveled to hell to be tormented by the souls he had wronged. After Clarence prays for his family's welfare, he falls asleep; Brakenbury then enters and speaks a few words about the glory of princes, to be followed in by the two Murderers, who present their warrant.

After Brakenbury and the Keeper leave, the Murderers have second thoughts about their deed when they remember Judgment Day. They regain their resolve thinking about the reward that Richard will give them, with the Second Murderer ruminating on the eternal nagging of the conscience —and losing his resolve again. Clarence awakes, and the two men inform him that they have come on behalf of King Edward to kill him. Clarence pleads that he deserves no harm from them, having never done them harm, but the men invoke the authority of King Edward—which Clarence insists should be ignored if it contradicts the authority of God. But the Murderers point out that Clarence forsook his oath to serve King Henry VI, leaving Clarence to question how Edward, for whose sake he rebelled against Henry, can be justified in ordering his murder. The Murderers inform Clarence that Gloucester—who had correctly anticipated Clarence's pleading—was no ally of his. Clarence continues to plead, and the Second Murderer hesitates, but the First Murderer finally manages to stab Clarence. He then takes Clarence away to throw him in a wine cask, while the Second Murderer repents.

Act 2, Scene 1

King Edward delights in the peacemaking he has accomplished among the various courtly parties before him, including Hastings, Rivers, Dorset, Buckingham, and Queen Elizabeth. When Richard arrives, he likewise speaks out in a grand and lofty style on behalf of making peace. Queen Elizabeth then suggests that Clarence should be shown mercy, at which Richard announces that Clarence has died in prison. When Stanley arrives in an untimely fashion to beg clemency for his servant, who committed murder, Edward laments that no one had seen fit to beg him to show clemency to Clarence, as Clarence had done him so much service. When King Edward expresses fear of God's retribution and departs with others, Richard voices to Buckingham his suspicion that Queen Elizabeth and her kin ordered Clarence's death.

Act 2, Scene 2

At the palace, the old Duchess of York, mother of King Edward, Richard, and Clarence, is talking to Clarence's son and daughter about his death and Edward's sickness. The children inform their grandmother that Richard has blamed Edward for Clarence's death, which the Duchess disputes. Queen Elizabeth then enters to relate that King Edward has just died. The Duchess expresses her grief over the deaths of the two virtuous images of her husband, with only the "false glass" of Richard remaining alive. At length, the children mourn their father's death, Queen Elizabeth mourns her husband's death, and the Duchess mourns both deaths.

Richard, Buckingham, and others arrive to announce a plan to send a small party to bring the deceased king's son, also named Edward, to London. Buckingham and Rivers voice their concern over the fragility of the rule of such a young man. Expressing his own hopes of maintaining peace, Richard sends Queen Elizabeth and his mother to fetch the young prince. Buckingham then reveals that he intends to help Richard turn Queen Elizabeth's kin against young Edward.

Act 2, Scene 3

Three Citizens gather and speak of political matters. Knowing that King Edward is dead, they wonder how effectively the young prince will rule. The Third Citizen points out that both Queen Elizabeth's kin and Richard might conspire to gain the throne. The First Citizen voices some optimism, but the others have little hope that peace will hold.

Act 2, Scene 4

The Duchess of York and Queen Elizabeth wonder at how much Prince Edward has grown, especially in relation to his brother the sprouting Duke of York. York remarks that Richard had told him that weeds grow quickly, flowers slowly; the Duchess remarks that Richard grew slowly but was certainly no flower, and York relates a jest he might have made at Richard's expense. A Messenger then arrives to announce that Rivers, Grey, and Sir Thomas Vaughan have been taken prisoner, leading Queen Elizabeth to be alarmed at the coming ruin of her house. The Duchess despairs, and Queen Elizabeth and the young York head for sanctuary.

Act 3, Scene 1

Richard and Buckingham welcome Prince Edward, who is weary with travel and grief over his deceased uncles. Richard assures him that they died for being false friends, which Edward doubts. Edward greets the Mayor and Citizens kindly, then wonders why his mother and brother have not arrived; Hastings then enters to note that the two have taken sanctuary, and Buckingham denounces Queen Elizabeth's peevishness and asks the Cardinal to fetch York. The Cardinal objects, but Buckingham convinces him that to do so would not be a violation of the laws of sanctuary.

Richard suggests to Prince Edward that he lodge at the Tower, which was built by Julius Caesar. Prince Edward contemplates the nature of fame and determines that he will someday attempt to conquer France. The Cardinal returns with York, who then parries wits with his uncle. At length, Richard persuades York and Prince Edward to proceed to the Tower; when they depart, Buckingham remarks that Queen Elizabeth must have incited York to be insolent. He then asks Catesby whether Hastings will join them in their plot to gain Richard's coronation as king. Catesby leaves to probe Hastings while informing him of the impending execution of Queen Elizabeth's kin, Hastings's enemies; Richard asserts that Hastings will be beheaded if he does not cooperate.

Act 3, Scene 2

At the house of Hastings, a messenger arrives from Lord Stanley, who dreamt that he was beheaded by Richard, "the boar," and is concerned over the meetings of the separated councils. Hastings tells the messenger that Stanley need not worry, as Catesby will inform him of goings-on at the alternate council.

Catesby arrives and tells Hastings of the impending executions, and Hastings rejoices—but remarks that he would never support Richard's coronation as king, leading Catesby to comment in an aside about Hastings's impending execution. Stanley then arrives and expresses his concern in person, which Hastings dismisses. Hastings then tells a Pursuivant (a royal messenger) of his delight in the execution of Queen Elizabeth's kin, and he holds brief counsel with a priest. Buckingham then fetches Hastings to dine—and die—at the Tower.

Act 3, Scene 3

At Pomfret Castle, Ratcliffe leads Rivers, Grey, and Vaughan to their deaths. Rivers and Grey lament the fulfillment of Margaret's curses.

Act 3, Scene 4

A number of lords are dining at the Tower and planning the date of Edward's coronation, with Hastings declaring that he will speak on behalf of Richard in his absence. Richard then arrives; after sending the Bishop of Ely to fetch him some strawberries, Richard learns from Buckingham of Hastings's unwillingness to join their plot. Richard and Buckingham exit, leaving Hastings to assert that Richard is evidently in good spirits. When the two men return, Richard complains that Queen Elizabeth and Jane Shore, Edward's mistress, had practiced witchcraft against him, crippling his arm. Hastings utters a comment that Richard insists is a treasonous defense of Shore and declares that Hastings will be immediately beheaded. Hastings, too, laments the fulfillment of Margaret's curse.

Act 3, Scene 5

At the Tower, Richard and Buckingham greet the Mayor with a display of paranoia over traitors. When Hastings's head is brought in, Richard declares that Hastings had been associating with Shore, and Buckingham says that Hastings had been plotting their murders. They express regret that their supporters had seen fit to execute Hastings so hastily, as the Mayor could not then hear his guilty testimony. The Mayor believes them and departs, and Richard tells Buckingham to go to London and persuade the people that Edward's line is corrupted with bastardy. Meanwhile, Richard will have holy men join him at Baynard's Castle and remarks that he will have Clarence's children confined to solitude.

Act 3: Scene 6

The Scrivener who copied the indictment of

Hastings notes that the entire episode seems tainted with treachery, but he knows better than to put his own life at risk by saying anything.

Act 3, Scene 7

At Baynard's Castle, Buckingham reports to Richard that he managed to convince some people that the late King Edward was himself a bastard child and that Richard should be named king instead of Prince Edward. The response to his assertions was unenthusiastic, but the idea was established nevertheless.

Richard then enters the castle, while Buckingham will pretend to be seeking an audience with him but having difficulty. Catesby acts as messenger, telling Buckingham in the Mayor's presence that Richard's religious duties are his priority; Buckingham then comments pointedly about Richard's piety, in contrast to the late Edward's purported adultery. After Catesby goes back inside, Richard appears in the presence of two Bishops and asks why Buckingham and the others have sought him there. Buckingham declares that Richard would be doing the nation good service by accepting the crown, but Richard humbly refuses, saying that he has no ambition to rule the nation and that Prince Edward will prove a perfectly capable leader. Buckingham insists, noting there are serious doubts about Prince Edward's legitimacy as heir to the throne. Richard refuses, Buckingham expresses severe disappointment, and the Mayor and the others leave; Richard then has Catesby call them back, and he tells them that he will accept the kingship for the good of the nation after all. Buckingham announces that the coronation should take place tomorrow, and Richard retires with the Bishops.

Act 4, Scene 1

The Duchess of York, Queen Elizabeth, and Anne cross paths at the Tower. There, Brakenbury informs Queen Elizabeth that Richard—whom he calls first king, then Lord Protector—has disallowed any contact with the Princes Edward and York. Stanley then arrives, sent by Richard to bring Anne to be crowned queen, and Queen Elizabeth mourns that Margaret's curse is coming to pass; she urges her son Dorset to flee to join Richmond, the stepson of Stanley, in Breton (Brittany), France. Before leaving with Stanley, Anne regrets that she allowed herself to be wooed by the man who killed her husband; in fact, since she cursed whoever would be Richard's wife, she cursed herself. Before again heading for sanctuary, Queen Elizabeth bids the Tower's stones keep her sons safe.

Act 4, Scene 2

After being helped to the throne by Buckingham, Richard eventually manages to tell him that he wishes that Prince Edward be slain. Buckingham asks for time to consider the order, and Richard immediately loses confidence in

Buckingham and instead asks a page if he knows anyone who would commit murder for a fair reward; the page suggests a man named Tyrrel. Stanley arrives to report that Dorset has fled to the aid of Richmond. Richard then tells Catesby to spread rumors that Anne is grievously ill and declares that he intends to find a lowly mate for Clarence's daughter while he himself will marry King Edward and Queen Elizabeth's daughter. Tyrrel arrives, and Richard orders him to kill Edward and York. Buckingham then returns, and while Richard muses over the threat of Richmond, Buckingham boldly and repeatedly asks for the earldom of Hereford, which Richard had promised him. When Richard refuses, Buckingham resolves to flee.

Act 4, Scene 3

Tyrrel reveals that two men murdered the princes on his behalf—and afterward regretted doing so. After receiving this news, Richard reveals that Clarence's children have been dealt with and that Anne has also passed away. Richard then notes that he would woo Elizabeth, daughter of Queen Elizabeth, in part because Richmond might otherwise do so in a ploy to gain the throne. Ratcliffe arrives to announce that the Bishop of Ely has fled to Richmond and that Buckingham is rallying an army of rebellious Welshmen.

Act 4, Scene 4

Queen Margaret, slinking about the palace, happens upon the grieving Queen Elizabeth and Duchess of York. Margaret eventually approaches the women as if to extend sympathy, but instead she rejoices in their sorrows, which she sees as fitting retribution for the wrongs she herself has suffered. She castigates the Duchess for having given birth to Richard, who has brought about so many deaths. Elizabeth wishes only to learn how to issue curses from Margaret, but she merely turns and departs.

King Richard then appears, to be intercepted by the two women. He initially has his trumpeters drown out their chiding, but the Duchess demands an audience; she prophecies that Richard will die in battle, with his enemies heartened by the souls of King Edward's slain children. Queen Elizabeth starts to leave after the Duchess, but Richard asks her to stay and inquires of her daughter, also named Elizabeth. Queen Elizabeth declares that she would sooner damage her own self by declaring that someone other than King Edward was the girl's father than allow her to be used—or killed—for Richard's advantage. At length, Richard admits that he wishes to marry young Elizabeth, but Queen Elizabeth doubts that his love is genuine and asks how he could actually woo her, given all of their family members whose deaths he ordered. Still, Richard describes how Queen Elizabeth could regain her former stature and rebuild her family by endorsing the match; in place of the sons she lost, she would be blessed with royal grandchildren. Queen Elizabeth resists, offering various objections to the match; when Richard begins to swear an oath, she points out that he has already forsaken all sacred people and things and thus has no one and nothing to swear on. Still, Richard insists that only a union between himself and Elizabeth can bring peace to the nation, and Queen Elizabeth at last relents and goes to speak to her daughter.

Ratcliffe arrives to inform Richard that Richmond's navy is awaiting the help of Buckingham's army on the western coast. Richard seems confused in giving orders to Catesby and Ratcliffe. Stanley arrives and confirms that Richmond is at sea, presumably on his way to ally with Dorset and Buckingham and seek the crown. Stanley assures Richard that his loyalty lies with him, not with his own stepson, and so Richard bids him to raise troops in the north—while another of Stanley's sons, George Stanley, will be held hostage.

Two Messengers arrive to report that various lords are up in arms, but a Third Messenger reports that Buckingham's army is scattered, and a Fourth Messenger declares that Richmond's navy has been dispersed by a storm. Finally, Catesby arrives to report that Buckingham has been taken and that Richmond has landed at Milford.

Act 4, Scene 5

Stanley sends Sir Christopher to tell his stepson Richmond that he cannot send aid while his other son is being held by Richard but also that Queen Elizabeth has consented to give Richmond her daughter's hand. Sir Christopher notes that Richmond has already been joined by a number of valiant soldiers.

Act 5, Scene 1

As he is led to his execution, Buckingham expresses remorse for his role in Richard's rise to the throne and admits that he deserves the punishment he is receiving.

Act 5, Scene 2

At Richmond's camp, Richmond announces that they are receiving reinforcements from Stanley and condemns Richard's bloody tyranny, which brings words of support from Oxford, Blunt, and Herbert.

Act 5, Scene 3

At Bosworth Field, Richard's tent is pitched, and Norfolk assures Richard that Richmond's rebel army is only a third of the size of the royal army. Meanwhile, Richmond dispatches Blunt with a note for Stanley and retires to his own tent to discuss strategy. In turn, Richard dispatches Catesby to bid Stanley to join them before sunrise; Richard then asks for wine, inquires as to the melancholy Northumberland, and confesses to being somewhat low in spirits. At length, he sleeps. Stanley then arrives at Richmond's tent to assure him that he will offer his aid in the coming battle; however, with his son's life at stake, Stanley cannot be too obvious in his support. Richmond prays for his soldiers and likewise falls asleep.

As the two men lie unconscious, the ghosts of Richard's many victims—including King Henry VI, Henry's son Edward, Clarence, Rivers, Grey, Vaughan, Hastings, the young Princes Edward and York, Lady Anne, and Buckingham—pay them visits, all telling Richard to despair and die and telling Richmond that he should take heart and be victorious.

When Richard wakes, he frets over his afflicted conscience and realizes that he deserves the love of no one—and does not even love himself. He imagines that he dreamed the visits of the many ghosts. Ratcliffe then enters to rouse Richard to prepare for battle; fearing the desertion of his friends, Richard entreats Ratcliffe to join him in eavesdropping on their men. Richmond, too, then wakes, much heartened by the kindly visits from the ghosts that he seemed to have dreamed. He delivers an oration to his men, asserting that they are on the side of good, fighting against evil, and that Richard's allies, who certainly fear him and would rather not be ruled by him, are bound to desert him when confronted in battle.

Richard, meanwhile, is reassured as to his men's loyalty but despairs now at the fact that the sun will not shine that day. Norfolk reveals that he received a cryptic note, which Richard dismisses as a ruse by the enemy. Speaking to his own army, Richard denounces the rebels as unruly, greedy, pathetic vagabonds from France. A Messenger arrives to report that Stanley will not join them, and Richard demands the head of Stanley's son—but Norwich points out that the enemy is advancing, and they set off to battle.

Act 5, Scene 4

In the heat of the battle, Catesby seeks help for Richard, who has fought fiercely even on foot. Having slain five of Richmond's doubles, Richard exclaims that he would give his kingdom for a horse.

Act 5, Scene 5

Richmond slays Richard. Having taken the crown from the deceased King Richard's head, Stanley turns it over to Richmond. Stanley notes that his son George has fortunately not been killed. Richmond declares that in marrying young Elizabeth, he will at last be uniting his own house of Lancaster with Elizabeth's house of York, ending the civil strife that has long plagued the nation.

Characters

Lady Anne

As the widow of Edward, Prince of Wales, who was the son and heir of King Henry VI, Anne hates Richard for murdering her husband and father-in-law, but Richard charms her into marrying him. As Richard's unhappy queen, she dies of unstated causes after he tires of her. Anne first appears following the coffin of her father-in-law, Henry VI. She laments King Henry's death and curses his murderer, Richard, and also places a curse on any woman who marries Richard—thus, ironically, cursing herself. When Richard enters and halts the funeral procession, Anne disgustedly calls him a "foul devil" and begs for lightning to strike him dead. But Richard is persistent: he flatters Anne and excuses his crimes by asserting that he was inspired by her beauty, claims he loves her, and even invites her to kill him with his own sword. Eventually, Anne relents. "I would I knew thy heart," she tells him before agreeing to accept his ring.

In acknowledging how implausible this scene is, critics have attempted to show how Richard successfully woos Anne. He carefully listens to her, observes her changing emotions, and adapts his arguments to these changes, eventually winning her sympathy. He plays upon Anne's grief and skillfully manipulates her. Some critics argue that, in addition to being in mourning, Anne is susceptible to Richard's advances simply because she behaves as women were expected to at the time.

Media Adaptations

- A critically acclaimed motion picture version of *Richard III* was produced and directed by Laurence Olivier in 1955 through London Film Productions. The film features Olivier himself, John Gielgud, Ralph Richardson, and Claire Bloom. The film was distributed on video by Embassy Home Entertainment in 1985.

- The British Broadcasting Corporation and Time-Life Television produced a televised performance of *The Tragedy of Richard the Third* in 1983, as part of the "Shakespeare Plays" series on PBS.

- Another motion picture version of *Richard III* was directed by Richard Loncraine and produced by Metro-Goldwyn-Mayer/United Artists in 1995; it was set in an imaginary England of the 1930s, capturing the political atmosphere of instability and tyranny of the play's true historical time period. Ian McKellen, who wrote the screenplay, fills the role of Richard III, with other stars including Annette Bening as Queen Elizabeth, Jim Broadbent as Buckingham, Robert Downey Jr. as Rivers, Nigel Hawthorne as Clarence, Kristin Scott Thomas as Anne, and Maggie Smith as the Duchess of York.

- Al Pacino's 1996 *Looking for Richard* is a unique film, mixing documentary interviews about the play with scholars, critics, actors, and people on the street with fully costumed and staged scenes from the play. Pacino directed, cowrote the narration with Frederic Kimball, and stars as Richard III. Winona Ryder is Lady Anne, Alec Baldwin is Clarence, and Kevin Spacey is Buckingham. Estelle Parsons is the

When Anne appears for the next and last time, in act 4, scene 1, she has married Richard and is miserable. She recalls the curse she had made on any woman "mad" enough to become his wife and bitterly laments, "Within so small a time, my woman's heart *Grossly grew captive to his honey words,* And prov'd the subject of mine own soul's curse." She goes unwillingly to Westminster to be crowned Richard's queen. Richard later starts a rumor that Anne is seriously ill, then later still he briefly mentions that she has died.

Traditionally, Anne has been regarded as weak and vain for being fooled by Richard's flattery. However, given Richard's powerful position as brother to King Edward and his demonstrated ruthlessness, Anne certainly cannot kill him and so has little choice but to accept him. Although her appearance in the play is fairly brief, Anne's role is important in that her encounter with Richard provides an early and revealing glimpse of his cunning and persuasiveness.

Boy and Daughter

Clarence's children, whose unmentioned names are Edward and Margaret, discuss their father's death with their grandmother, the Duchess of York, revealing how thoroughly Richard had convinced them that King Edward was the one responsible.

Sir Robert Brakenbury

Brakenbury is Lieutenant of the Tower of London and in charge of the prison, where first the Duke of Clarence and later King Edward's two young sons are held.

Sir William Catesby

As a supporter of Richard, Catesby is sent to find out whether Hastings will support Richard's coronation and manages to probe and advise the lord without revealing his own relationship to the aspiring usurper. Catesby also assists in Richard's deceptive posing as a man of religion at Baynard's Castle and, during the battle on Bosworth Field, calls out for the rescue of the frantic King Richard.

Citizens

Three Citizens discuss the death of King Edward IV and their low expectations with regard to the country's future, demonstrating the opinions of the common people.

Marquis of Dorset

Dorset is Queen Elizabeth's son from a previous marriage. He joins the Earl of Richmond's side after Richard is crowned king.

King Edward IV

Edward IV is the king of England at the play's opening. Edward is ill at the beginning of the play, and his only substantial activity is the peacemaking he accomplishes among his courtly followers and his wife's family. After Richard appears and declares that King Edward's pardon for their brother, the Duke of Clarence, came too late to save him from death, he laments that no one advised him to be merciful earlier. He then marches off and later dies.

Duke of Buckingham

Buckingham is Richard's primary coconspirator. He helps Richard become king but falls out of favor when he balks at murdering Edward IV's two young sons. He joins the Earl of Richmond's side against Richard but is later captured and executed. Serving as Richard's right-hand man, Buckingham plays an important role in the play. Richard uses him as an adviser and a spy and in fact calls him "my other self" in act 2, scene 2.

Buckingham's first appearances give no indication that he is anything other than a minor character; Richard refers to him merely as one of several "simple gulls" or fools whom he is deceiving in act 1, scene 3. Once King Edward dies, Buckingham gains prominence, as he schemes to place the king's heir—Edward, Prince of Wales—in Richard's power by fetching the child to London without the protection of his mother or her kinsmen.

When Queen Elizabeth flees to sanctuary with her youngest son, the Duke of York, Buckingham takes it upon himself to order the child brought back to London.

In act 3, scene 5, Buckingham asserts that he is nearly as good an actor as Richard is: "I can counterfeit the deep tragedian," he says, as he and Richard prepare to fool the Mayor of London into believing that Richard is a good man who has been cruelly betrayed. He insists, "Ghastly looks *Are at my service, like enforceèd smiles;* And both are ready in their offices / At any time to grace my stratagems." He proves his point well in scene 7 when he helps Richard stage so convincing a performance of pious humility and reluctant royal worth that the citizens of London entreat Richard to become king.

Still, Buckingham falls short of being Richard's "other self" when it comes to murdering the two young princes. In act 4, scene 2, the newly crowned Richard first hints then bluntly states that he wants King Edward's heirs killed. Buckingham's reply—"Your Grace may do your pleasure"—does not satisfy Richard, who needs a perpetrator for a crime so heinous. Buckingham's next attempt to postpone making a decision only infuriates Richard, who mutters, "High-reaching Buckingham grows circumspect." Later, when Buckingham returns to the question of the princes' murder—as well as that of the earldom he hoped to earn through his treachery—Richard dismisses him. Buckingham's hesitation costs him his life. Although similar to

Richard, having likewise been described as a machiavel, ultimately Buckingham is no match for his deceitful king.

Edward, Prince of Wales

The Prince of Wales is the young son and heir of King Edward IV. Along with his younger brother, the Duke of York, he is led to—and imprisoned in—the Tower of London by his ambitious uncle Richard. Later both children are murdered on Richard's orders.

Queen Elizabeth

Formerly Lady Grey, she is the wife of King Edward IV and the mother of Edward, Prince of Wales, and Richard, Duke of York, the King's two young heirs. She shows a certain familial affiliation for Richard at first—supporting Richard's schoolyard-style deflection of Margaret's curse on him, confirming, "Thus have you breathed your curse against yourself"—but ultimately Queen Elizabeth hates Richard for murdering her brother and her sons. Nevertheless, he persuades her to consider him as a mate for her daughter, Elizabeth. Queen Elizabeth's presence and comments generally highlight Richard's ruthless quest for the throne, since, as King Edward's wife and the mother of the heir, she has perhaps the most direct interest in Richard's success or failure. As early as the first scene, Richard is seen spreading lies regarding her influence over King Edward, revealing that Queen

Elizabeth and her relatives are operating as a distinct faction in the context of the court.

Queen Elizabeth first enters in act 1, scene 3, voicing her fears about the king's illness to her brother, Lord Rivers, and her two older sons, Lord Grey and the Marquis of Dorset. She knows that if King Edward dies, her young son Edward, Prince of Wales, the heir to the throne, could be placed under Richard's protection, "a man," she tells her sons and brother, "that loves not me, nor none of you"; indeed, Richard appears shortly afterward and insults her.

In act 2, scene 1, Queen Elizabeth and her kinsmen reconcile with Richard and other members of the court at King Edward's request. But by scene 2, he is dead, and the distraught Queen Elizabeth agrees with Richard that the Prince of Wales should be brought to court. By scene 4, her situation has worsened, as Richard has imprisoned Rivers and Grey, and also holds the Prince of Wales in his custody. Queen Elizabeth realizes that Richard now controls the government, remarking, "Insulting tyranny begins to jut / Upon the innocent and aweless throne." She flees with her youngest son, York, into sanctuary, but Richard and Buckingham order York brought back to London to "lodge" in the Tower with the Prince of Wales, and in act 4, scene 1, Elizabeth is barred from visiting them.

Elizabeth's final and most famous encounter with Richard occurs in act 4, scene 4, when she apparently agrees to persuade her daughter to marry him. This scene has been described as a battle of wits between Richard and Elizabeth, and it is not clear who wins. Elizabeth never explicitly states that she will tell her daughter to marry him. Instead she asks, "Shall I go win my daughter to thy will?" and ends by telling Richard, "I go. Write to me very shortly, / And you shall understand from me her mind." In act 4, scene 5, we are told that she has promised her daughter to the Earl of Richmond. Has Elizabeth been weak-willed and inconsistent, or has she finally outwitted Richard?

George, Duke of Clarence

Clarence is the brother of King Edward IV and Richard. He is imprisoned in the Tower of London after Richard turns King Edward against him, never realizing that Richard is his enemy. The dream that he relates to the Keeper is filled with vivid metaphorical imagery that conveys the sense of doom eventually closing over many of the play's characters. When Richard sends assassins to the Tower, Clarence nearly persuades them not to kill him, but the more determined of the two eventually stabs him.

Ghosts

Among the Ghosts who visit King Richard and Richmond on the night before the battle at Bosworth are Edward, Prince of Wales, Henry VI's son, who was stabbed by Richard; King Henry VI, who was murdered by Richard; Clarence; Rivers, Grey, and Vaughan; Hastings; the young princes

Edward and York; Lady Anne; and Buckingham.

Lord Grey

Lord Grey is Queen Elizabeth's son from a previous marriage; Richard has him assassinated.

Lord Hastings

Sometimes called Lord Chamberlain, Hastings is assassinated for expressing that he would not support Richard's ambition to be king.

Henry, Earl of Richmond

Henry, known in the plays as Richmond, is a Lancastrian who raises an army to defeat King Richard III and end his reign of tyranny. Although he is the play's hero, Richmond's role is minimal; he interacts with other characters very little, giving only a few substantial speeches on his way to slaying Richard and gaining the throne to become Henry VII.

Queen Margaret

Margaret is the widow of King Henry VI, who was murdered by Richard. She prophesies revenge for herself and destruction for King Edward IV's family and supporters. Margaret appears in only two scenes, but her influence is felt throughout the play. She first enters in act 1, scene 3, speaking—as she often does—in asides, commenting to the audience on the bickering among her Yorkist enemies, including Queen Elizabeth and her kinsmen, Richard, Clarence, and the various lords. When Margaret finally speaks directly to those present, she curses them, foretelling misery to Elizabeth and death to Rivers and Hastings, reserving her most virulent words for Richard. By the time she appears again in act 4, scene 4, most of her prophecies have been fulfilled. She exults in her revenge and gives Queen Elizabeth and the Duchess of York some brief advice about how to curse Richard, who has become, as Margaret had predicted, an enemy to all of them.

When *Richard III* is produced onstage, Margaret's role is frequently omitted on the grounds that the language in her scenes is too formal and repetitive to have an impact on modern audiences. On the other hand, Margaret provides useful background information on Richard's grim quest for power. Her predictions and ghostlike presence—in act 4 she states, "Here in these confines slily have I lurk'd / To watch the waning of mine enemies"—reinforce the theme of divine retribution in the play, as do the characters' recollections of her prophecies when they are led to their executions. In act 3, scene 4, for example, Hastings laments, "O Margaret, Margaret, now thy heavy curse / Is lighted on poor Hastings' wretched head." Likewise, in act 5, scene 1, Buckingham cries, "Thus Margaret's curse falls heavy on my neck."

Lord Mayor of London

The Lord Mayor is the leader of the citizens of London. After the death of King Edward IV, Richard and Buckingham deceptively convince him that Richard deserves to become king.

Murderers

The Two Murderers sent to dispose of Clarence manage to do so only after some hesitation resulting from moral qualms about the act.

Sir Richard Ratcliffe

Ratcliffe provides crucial information regarding the activities of King Richard III's enemies.

Richard, Duke of Gloucester

The younger brother of King Edward IV and George, Duke of Clarence, Richard later becomes King Richard III. The play's opening couplet ("Now is the winter of our discontent / Made glorious summer by this son of York") and the final line of act 5, scene 4 ("A horse! A horse! My kingdom for a horse!") are probably the most famous lines in the play; appropriately, they are also the first and the last words that Richard speaks. Richard is the energizing force of the play and is responsible for most of its dark comedy, which usually occurs when he is mocking himself or ridiculing his victims. He has been called a machiavel—one who views politics as outside of morality and will use any means, however unscrupulous, to achieve political power—because of his ruthless drive for power. Almost as soon as he appears onstage he tells us that he is "determined to prove a villain" and mentions the traps he is setting against his own brothers. He describes himself as "deform'd, unfinish'd," and so unpleasant to look at that dogs bark at him, and he blames his wickedness on his physical appearance. One scholar has noted that explicit connections were indeed drawn between external appearance and internal character in Shakespeare's time.

Richard does not announce his intention to become king until act 3, scene 1, but his plots and murders ever lead in that direction, and in act 4 he is finally crowned. A focus of critical debate has been whether Richard himself truly controls events or whether he is simply a divine instrument meant to clear England of the corruption of civil war so that the country can begin afresh. In either case, toward the end of the play Richard has definitely lost control as well as his sense of humor; in act 5, scene 3, he notes, "I have not that alacrity of spirit / Nor cheer of mind that I was wont to have." The night before battle, he is tormented by sleeplessness and haunted by the ghosts of those he has murdered. The following day he is killed in battle by Richmond.

A frequent topic of discussion is the apparent contradiction between Richard's monstrous behavior and his continuing attractiveness to audiences. One argument suggests that he is not meant to be a realistic character but a melodramatic, comic villain whose extreme antics lighten the mood of what would otherwise be an unendurably morbid play. A somewhat different view holds that Richard's witty dialogue and his ability to mock himself lead audiences to disassociate him from the many murders that he orders but does not himself commit; the murders that he did commit occur before the action of *Richard III*.

It has also been argued that—with the exception of the two young princes—Richard's victims are not as innocent as they seem but are instead hypocrites who know they are being used and who try unsuccessfully to use Richard. According to this view, Richard is simply more clever than anyone else in the play at getting what he wants.

Richard, Duke of York

The younger son of King Edward IV and thus second in line to the throne when his father dies, York demonstrates a certain cleverness in act 2, scene 4, and parries wits with Richard in act 3, scene 1. He is imprisoned in the Tower along with his elder brother by their ambitious uncle Richard, who later has them murdered.

Earl Rivers

Rivers is Queen Elizabeth's brother; Richard has him assassinated.

Scrivener

In discussing the indictment of Hastings that he copied, the scrivener demonstrates how poorly Richard is disguising his foul deeds.

Lord Stanley, Earl of Derby

Stanley is the Earl of Richmond's stepfather. Stanley demonstrates loyalty to Richard but is distrusted by him because he is related to the primary threat to Richard's rule. As king, Richard takes Stanley's son George as hostage, hoping to ensure that Stanley will not dare to fight on Richmond's side. Stanley manages to prevent Richard from realizing that he is indeed supporting his stepson until just before the battle, when Richard has no time to have Stanley's son executed.

Sir James Tyrrel

Tyrrel is recruited by Richard to arrange for the murder of the two young heirs of Edward IV. His brief soliloquy on that heinous crime serves to highlight Richard's evil.

Sir Christopher Urswick

Urswick is a chaplain who sends a letter to Richmond on behalf of Stanley. He also informs Stanley of other supporters of Richmond.

Duchess of York

The Duchess of York is the mother of King Edward IV, of George, Duke of Clarence, and of Richard. She mourns the deaths of King Edward and Clarence and curses Richard for his wickedness. After long inhabiting a passive role, commenting only offhand on her low opinion of the youngest of her three sons, she manages to vehemently curse Richard after gaining inspiration from Margaret.

Succession

In act 2, scene 3, of *Richard III*, a group of English citizens worries over what will become of the nation now that King Edward IV has died and his heir, Edward, Prince of Wales, is still a child. The citizens know that a Protector will be appointed to govern for Prince Edward until he is old enough to rule by himself. They also know that the child's uncles are vying with one another to be Protector, and the citizens are frightened that the inevitable power struggle will throw the country into turmoil. They have already endured a number of chaotic years in the course of the Wars of the Roses, as the Houses of York and Lancaster have fought back and forth for England's throne, and the citizens of England long for peace and order. Instead, of course, they get Richard.

The question of succession in English law, or the order—based on birth or marriage—by which a person lawfully and rightfully becomes monarch, was of much concern to the citizens of England during Shakespeare's time since their aging queen, Elizabeth I, was unmarried and had no heirs. Although Elizabeth was England's lawful queen, she had already weathered several challenges to her power, including those of Mary, Queen of Scots, a relative whom Elizabeth finally saw executed in

1587, and Philip II of Spain, who had sent his Armada in 1588 in hopes of unseating her. Thus, a play about an ambitious relative of a king who was determined to become king himself was very relevant to Shakespeare's audience.

Richard knows that he will in truth be a usurper: he will become king through illegal deeds and knows that if he does not at least *appear* to be England's lawful ruler, then he will suffer endless challenges to his power. The string of murders that Richard commits and orders before and after he becomes king can be seen as attempts to legitimize his rule by eliminating others with claims to the throne. Of the three brothers—King Edward IV; George, Duke of Clarence; and Richard, Duke of Gloucester—Richard is the youngest of the king's brothers and farthest from succession to the crown. Clarence is before him and might become the Protector of Edward's son and heir, the Prince of Wales, when King Edward dies. Thus, when King Edward falls seriously ill, Richard plots to have Clarence killed, removing in one stroke a possible Protector and a potential claimant to the throne.

Richard's next move is to make certain that he alone becomes Protector to his nephew, the Prince of Wales. He eliminates Rivers, who is the prince's uncle on his mother's side, and also murders Lord Grey, the prince's half-brother. (The prince's remaining half-brother, the Marquis of Dorset, escapes to join the Earl of Richmond.) Once Richard becomes the unchallenged Protector, he can more easily seize the throne for himself. He murders

Hastings after that nobleman swears to remain loyal to Prince Edward's right to the throne. By suggesting that the Prince of Wales and his younger brother, the Duke of York, are illegitimate and not true sons of Edward IV, and are therefore unqualified for succession, Richard and Buckingham convince the citizens that Richard is the only one left who, by lineage and virtue, deserves to be king.

Even after Richard becomes king, he knows that his power is vulnerable to challenge as long as the Prince of Wales and the Duke of York remain alive; although imprisoned and hidden from sight, these two rightful heirs to King Edward's throne could still serve as a rallying point for dissatisfied or ambitious subjects. So Richard adds the two young princes to his list of victims; still, he does not feel secure. He imprisons Clarence's son because that child has a better claim to the throne than he, and he marries off Clarence's daughter to a commoner to destroy any possibility of royal claimants coming from that blood line. Finally, Richard hears that his enemy the Lancastrian Earl of Richmond intends to marry Edward IV's daughter Elizabeth and thus unite the royal families of York and Lancaster. Richard hopes to prevent this union and strengthen his own claim to the throne by marrying King Edward's daughter himself, which is why he tries to persuade Queen Elizabeth to consent to such a marriage. Richard's attempts to legitimize his power through bloodshed end when he is killed in battle by the Earl of Richmond, who begins a new line of succession—the Tudors—and is crowned Henry

Retributive Justice

Widespread in Shakespeare's era was the idea that the members of the court of King Edward IV, inhabiting their positions of power and advantage only as a result of earlier bloodshed and sin, met their downfall as a result of divinely ordained retributive justice—justice that paid them back for what they had done. Based on the prominent references to that notion in *Richard III*, especially as represented in the curses issued by Margaret. E. M. Y. Tillyard goes as far as to assert, "The play's main end is to show the working out of God's will in English history." Coppélia Kahn, in turn, descriptively notes, "Critics have often interpreted *Richard III* as the lump of chaos born of England's chaos, the incarnation of its untrammeled slaughter of sons, brothers, fathers."

Indeed, Shakespeare calls much attention to the notion of God dispensing justice among those who have committed crimes or misdeeds. In his essay, "Angel with Horns," A. P. Rossiter points out that Raphael Holinshed, the author of one of Shakespeare's sources, makes reference to the notion of such justice and that the playwright then incorporated that notion throughout *Richard III*. In terms of the scenes, several are devoted explicitly to lamentations over those lost, with Margaret offering Queen Elizabeth this conclusion in act 4, scene 4: "Thus hath the course of justice whirled about / And left thee but a very prey to time." In terms of the language, Shakespeare often has characters repeating lines or responding to each other in back-and-forth patterns, suggesting what Rossiter dubs a "tennis-court game of rhetoric" that reflects the equality of payback.

Above all, Rossiter highlights "the simple overriding principle derived from the Tudor historians: that England rests under a chronic curse —the curse of faction, civil dissension, and fundamental anarchy, resulting from the deposition and murder of the Lord's Anointed (Richard II) and the usurpation of the house of Lancaster." This curse, which issued forth originally from the mouth of Richard II and is later echoed in *Richard III* by Queen Margaret, is of course ultimately enacted by God alone. Perhaps ironically, then, God proves to enact these curses through the character of Richard III. Regarding Richard's paradoxical status, Rossiter concludes,

> He is not only this demon incarnate, he is in effect God's agent in a predetermined plan of divine retribution: the "scourge of God." Now by Tudor-Christian historical principles, this plan is *right*. Thus, in a real sense, Richard is a king who "can do no wrong"; for in the pattern of the justice of divine retribution on the wicked, he functions as an avenging angel.

Richard's evil, then, was in a sense "good."

Shakespeare seems to have also weighted the notion of retributive justice by not including certain scenes that might have served to inspire greater sympathy in the audience. August Wilhelm von Schlegel suggests, "Shakespeare intended that terror rather than compassion should prevail throughout this tragedy: he has rather avoided than sought the pathetic scenes which he had at command." Schlegel points out that the death of Clarence alone is depicted onstage, with the deaths of Anne and the young princes only mentioned; meanwhile, characters such as Hastings, Buckingham, and Rivers are not presented in ways that might inspire the audience to pity them. The overall effect, then, is that the audience is fairly indifferent, if not content, when many of these characters are eliminated; as such, the audience more readily agrees with the notion that these characters are being punished by God for their sins and for the sins of their forebears. Schlegel concludes, "Shakespeare has most accurately observed poetical justice in the genuine sense of the word, that is, as signifying the revelation of an invisible blessing or curse which hangs over human sentiments and actions."

Topics for Further Study

- King Richard III was one of the most ruthless politicians ever to grace England's royal throne, ordering numerous murders to ensure that no one could be considered to have a more legitimate claim to the throne than himself. In modern American politics, far different underhanded tactics are used by politicians to secure power. Write an essay on the American political tradition of mudslinging. Compare this tactic with the tactics used by Richard in moral terms, providing specific recent examples of mudslinging or other such competitive tactics that might be classified as immoral.

- As a Shakespearean villain and protagonist, Richard III has often been compared to Macbeth. Read *Macbeth* and write an essay in which you compare and contrast the two title characters.

- At least one critic has wondered why Shakespeare chose not to include the historical scene in which the Cardinal persuades Queen Elizabeth to release her son Richard, the Duke of York, from sanctuary (this occurs offstage in act 3, scene 1). Write a report on the concept of *sanctuary* in medieval law, discussing whether you believe the Cardinal should or should not have acted as ordered by Buckingham in not truly recognizing York's right to sanctuary.

- Identify a modern film in which the villain is not only the center of attention but also is depicted in a way that solicits the viewer's sympathy. In an essay, analyze the ways in which the director, writer, and actor in this film humanize the villain, comparing their methods with the theatrical strategies used by Shakespeare in *Richard III*. (If possible, also view a filmed version of *Richard III* and address the methods used by the actor playing the title character in your discussion.)

- The idea of retributive justice is still invoked in modern times. Write an essay about recent religious leaders who have claimed that events or occurrences signaled punishment from God. Analyze these leaders' motivations for making such claims and discuss reactions among various segments of the public. (For example, certain figures called the Indian Ocean tsunami of 2004 a retributive act of God.)

Style

Dark Comedy

A persistent thread of comedy runs through *Richard III.* Since the play is mostly about treachery and vengeance, the comedy it contains is appropriately dark, consisting of dramatic irony as well as parody. On the other hand, this comedy can be partly understood as intended to brighten the somber tone of that period of history. William E. Sheriff proposes that Shakespeare perhaps wished to enhance the last entry in his first group of four history plays from the plays of his competitors: "A cold-blooded approach to the throne, with no humor in Richard's character and, as a result, less interest, would have repeated the pattern of so many of the contemporary history plays." Some of Richard's humor comes from his self-ridicule, but much of it comes when he mocks the confidence that others mistakenly place in him.

Dramatic irony occurs when the audience understands the real significance of a character's words or actions but the character or those around him or her do not. Richard's sympathetic comments to his brother Clarence as he is being taken to prison constitute dramatic irony because the audience knows from Richard's opening soliloquy that he is responsible for Clarence's being jailed. Dramatic irony occurs again in act 3, scene 2, when Catesby suggests that Richard should be crowned king in lieu of the Prince of Wales, and Hastings declares: "I'll have this crown of mine cut from my shoulders / Before I'll see the crown so foul misplac'd." We already know from Richard's conversation with Buckingham one scene earlier that Hastings will indeed lose his head if he opposes Richard. Both of these incidents are intended to make the audience smile, if perhaps grimly, at Richard's trickery and his victims' naïveté.

Parody is the use of exaggerated imitation to ridicule someone or something that was meant to be taken seriously. Richard mocks both himself and Anne when he parodies a preening lover in act 1, after Anne—against all odds—accepts his ring: "I'll be at charges for a looking-glass, / And entertain a score or two of tailors / To study fashions to adorn my body." Part of the humor comes from Richard's ability to laugh at himself. Richard's most triumphant parody occurs when he fools the citizens of London into petitioning him to be their king. By imitating a holy man (which he most certainly is not) and appearing reluctant to accept the crown, Richard succeeds in getting the power he wants.

The Ultimate Actor

Richard's character is so central to *Richard III* that many commentators believe that the play in production is entirely dependent on that one role. For a play to revolve around a single role, that role must perhaps feature the utmost degree of dramatic complexity—and thus demand the utmost theatrical expertise. As quoted by Howard Staunton in *The Complete Illustrated Shakespeare*, Nathan Drake remarks of Richard,

> While to the explorer of the human mind he affords, by his penetration and address, a subject of peculiar interest and delight, he offers to the practised performer a study well calculated to call forth his fullest and finest exertions. He, therefore, whose histrionic powers are adequate to the just exhibition of this character, may be said to have attained the highest honours of his profession.

Indeed, in terms of character, Richard himself can be understood as first and foremost an impeccable actor.

A. P. Rossiter offers perhaps the most comprehensive discussion on Richard's theatricality. He first makes note of "the appeal of the actor: the talented being who can assume every mood and passion at will, at all events to the extent of making others believe in it." He then points out why the machinations of Richard, however wicked, prove so riveting: "The specific interest here is the *power* that would be in the hands of an actor consummate enough to make (quite literally) 'all the world a stage' and to work on humanity by the perfect simulation of every feeling." The art of self-presentation, in fact, might be considered the particular realm of both the actor and the politician.

Richard has so fine-tuned his ability to present himself that he is able to deceive and outmaneuver all others likewise seeking to claw their way to power.

The notion of the ultimate actor is closely related to the notion of the Superman, elaborated most extensively by the nineteenth-century German philosopher Friedrich Nietzsche. Nietzsche contended that the human being with complete control over his emotions and complete harnessing of his "will to power" could in effect out-evolve the rest of humanity, becoming a "Superman." Rossiter notes that Shakespeare, who predated Nietzsche by two hundred years, would have been exposed to the similar concepts of the Italian political theorist Niccolò Machiavelli in *The Prince*. Rossiter notes that Machiavelli's Prince and Shakespeare's Richard seek to embody the same quality: "a lifelong, unremitting vigilance in relentless simulation and impenetrable deception." Rossiter then invokes the language of Nietzsche, asserting, "There, precisely, lies the superhumanity of the Superman. The will-to-power is shorn of its effective power without it. He is an *artist* in evil." Richard, then, despite his ultimate downfall, was perhaps one of the greatest artists in superhumanity in history.

Curses and Prophecies

Language is a potent weapon in *Richard III*, particularly as a source of retribution. Prophecies and curses are delivered and fulfilled, while oaths that are sworn but later broken bring about disaster. Curses, prophecies, and false or imprudent oaths occur so frequently and are so powerful that they should be understood as having a profound effect on the play's outcome.

As early as act 1, scene 3, Margaret curses virtually every principal character in the play. She prays for the death of King Edward as well as his heirs and for a life of misery for Queen Elizabeth. She curses Hastings and Rivers with early death, Richard with sleepless nights and ruin. She finishes by prophesying that Buckingham will be betrayed by Richard: "O Buckingham, take heed of yonder dog! / Look when he fawns, he bites; and when he bites / His venom tooth will rankle to the death." By the end of the play, nearly all of Margaret's predictions and curses have been fulfilled.

Ironically, many of the characters bring destruction upon themselves by reinforcing Margaret's curses with their own false oaths and self-curses. For example, in act 4, scene 4, Richard swears to Queen Elizabeth that he loves her daughter, and he supports this oath with a self-curse that is meant to take effect if his oath proves false: "God and fortune, bar me happy hours! / Day, yield me not thy light, nor, night, thy rest!" Richard's oath is indeed false: he does not love Elizabeth's daughter but hopes to marry her to consolidate his power. His self-curse—ruin and sleepless nights—is identical to Margaret's curse in act 1, and by the end of the play, it is fulfilled.

Man or Monster?

The depiction of Richard III is without question the centerpiece of the play bearing his name, and in turn, the historical accuracy of that depiction—and whether Shakespeare actually sought to portray Richard accurately—has been much discussed. On this topic, John Julius Norwich observes, "King Richard III, the only English ruler since the Norman Conquest to have been killed in battle, is also the only one to have become a legend. That legend, due first to Sir Thomas More and then to Shakespeare, is that of the lame and twisted hunchback whose misshapen body reflects the evil heart within it." One problem is that the printing press was only just coming into use during Richard's lifetime, so historical records from his era are rare and hard to verify.

The ultimate source of most of the information used by Shakespeare—More's *Historie of King Richard the Thirde*—was written by a Tudor historian who was quite explicitly describing events from the point of view of Henry VII, the sovereign he was serving. As a result, some modern historians have conjectured that More portrayed Richard with emphasized if not exaggerated monstrosity. Robert Ornstein asserts that More describes Richard "as an explorer might describe a rare and horrifying species of poisonous snake. Never allowing his reader to savor Richard's histrionic performances, More makes each of Richard's successes an occasion for moral outrage, disgust, and scorn." Others have suggested that More demonstrated ample integrity both in other works and throughout his life, and that there is insufficient grounds for questioning his honesty with regard to his portrait of Richard. Norwich points out that More is "a formally canonized saint" in contending, "Nothing that we know of his character suggests that he would have … deliberately written what he knew in his heart to be untrue." Ultimately, no scholarly authority can determine with certainty the degree to which More was faithfully representing the villainy of Richard III.

Regardless of the accuracy of More's portrayal, Shakespeare chooses *not* to portray Richard as an utter monster. He also endows him with a variety of appealing characteristics. Ornstein declares that what Shakespeare does "is make Richard's perversity credible and, more than that, enjoyable, for the heartless murderer More depicts becomes in Shakespeare's play a humorist and a comedian so cheeky, frank, and enthusiastic in his wickedness that most of his betters seem unpardonably dishonest and dreary." Indeed, much of Richard's appeal comes from his sense of humor, a trait perhaps prized above all others by some entertainment-seeking audiences. William E. Sheriff asserts that, in this respect, the playwright perhaps sees Richard's comic depth and intelligence as necessities: "Shakespeare realized we had to put up with this fellow until we had him seated on the throne in order for the play to sustain interest." That is, if Richard had been portrayed as a mere caricature of a murderous villain, the play's central role might have lacked the desired level of psychological and dramatic tension.

Still, Shakespeare walks a fine line in his effort not to make Richard too likable. Norwich points out that the playwright leaves the audience understanding that Richard is responsible for Clarence's imprisonment and death. In his opening soliloquy, Richard boasts about how he had set Edward and Clarence at odds with each other, thus, in a sense, claiming responsibility for Clarence's arrest. Later, Richard is shown giving orders to the Murderers, whom he calls "my executioners," and the two subsequently declare that their "reward" will come from "the Duke of Gloucester's purse" and perform their deed uncertainly and as if illicitly. However, in reality, Clarence fully earned his detention in the Tower by, among other missteps, suggesting that Edward was illegitimate, and Edward did consequently condemn him to death. With respect to this major piece of the plot, Shakespeare does portray Richard as more evil than history indicates he was, if not as more monstrous.

Compare & Contrast

- **1470s:** The notion that God will exact revenge on those who participated in the usurping of King

Richard II's throne is in the forefront of the minds of those who are yet suffering through the Wars of the Roses.

1590s: Citizens of Elizabethan England trust that with the retributive justice brought about by King Richard III, peace may be likely to hold—but rebellions must still occasionally be put down.

Today: Wars and disasters are still invoked by some religious leaders as evidence that God is displeased with humankind.

- **1470s:** With written records scarce, people in positions of power can easily manipulate public perceptions of the truth by determining what information is made available.

  1590s: Written records are more available, making the falsification of historical events more difficult—but far from impossible.

  Today: While journalists and historians usually manage to ensure that people are made aware of historical truths, at least in more open societies, people in powerful political positions still have opportunities to manipulate public perceptions for their own ends.

- **1470s:** Murders are committed and

executions are ordered with fair regularity by both those who aspire to, and those who hold, England's royal throne.

1590s: Queen Elizabeth has maintained her reign for some thirty years, having survived several uprisings by Catholics looking to install her cousin, Mary, Queen of Scots—who is eventually executed.

Today: The last assassination of an American president was that of John F. Kennedy in 1963; among modern politicians, underhanded tactics are generally limited to slanderous mudslinging.

Sheriff, meanwhile, posits that even if Shakespeare softened Richard's monstrosity overall, he made an artistic decision to lessen Richard's appeal toward the end of the play, as demonstrated by his failure to sway Queen Elizabeth in act 4, scene 4, with his usual conversational ruses. Sheriff states of the playwright,

> It is my opinion that he wished to balance the presentation of his characterization of Richard; that is, whereas he first convinced us of the powers of this monstrous comedian, he now wishes to destroy that image in order that the entire concept of

Richard's character can be shattered on Bosworth Field without regret on the part of the spectator. The qualities we found fascinating in Richard, his brilliant wit, his corrupt sense of humor, his ability to stand outside the scene and watch himself, are missing in his encounter with Queen Elizabeth, and we are in this manner prepared for the concluding act of the play.

In other words, as a prelude to his well-deserved death, Shakespeare's Richard can be understood to demote himself from mesmerizing monster to a merely villainous man.

Critical Overview

Overwhelmingly, to be sure, critical attention to *Richard III* has focused on the title character. Indeed, as Mark Eccles notes, Richard speaks over a third of the plays' lines and appears in fourteen of twenty-five scenes—with five of his ten soliloquies occurring in the first three scenes—such that "his shadow hangs over the rest." Thus, the play as a total creation merits judgment based on the single portrait of King Richard III.

In that *Richard III* began life in performance, then, the actors who have inhabited the character of Richard deserve discussion in the context of critical opinion. Indeed, at the turn of the nineteenth century, Nathan Drake asserted that the play had gained renown largely by virtue of the portrayals of the title character: "The popularity of [*Richard III*], notwithstanding the moral enormity of its hero, may be readily accounted for, when we recollect that, the versatile and consummate hypocrisy of the tyrant has been embodied by the talents of such masterly performers as Garrick, Kemble, Cooke, and Kean." Regarding those men—all of whom graced the stage in the latter half of the eighteenth century or the beginning of the nineteenth—Eccles confirms that David Garrick was "the most brilliant actor of his time"; John Philip Kemble, as Richard, was "stately and eloquent"; and George Frederick Cooke made the villain "diabolical." Eccles offers especial praise for Edmund Kean, who distinguished himself as

Richard in London beginning in 1814. After citing Samuel Taylor Coleridge, who said that watching Kean was like "reading Shakespeare by flashes of lightning," and John Keats, who lauded the actor's "intense power of anatomizing the passions," Eccles offers his own assessment: "The play gave Kean chances to display the whole range of his virtuosity: his violent passions, his pantherlike gaiety, his energy and power. In the last act he held his audience spellbound. His awakening from his nightmare sent a shudder of terror through the spectators." Shakespeare is understood to have had Richard Burbage, one of the leading actors in his own company, in mind when he conceived of the role of King Richard III—and if the playwright had not had access to Burbage's talent, he might have written that role quite differently.

Regarding the role itself, A. P. Rossiter finds Richard to be "a huge triumphant stage personality, an early old masterpiece of the art of rhetorical stage writing, a monstrous being incredible in any sober, historical scheme of things." Similarly, Morton J. Frisch declares,

> Shakespeare has performed the extraordinary feat of presenting the serpentine wisdom of the tyrannic soul in such a way that it cannot fail to excite our sensibilities. In the satisfaction we receive in contemplating the character of Richard, in the various situations in which Shakespeare has shown him, it

is almost as if we lost sight of the cold-blooded, calculating tyrant whose ugly soul is overshadowed and even to some extent obscured by the marvelous play of his intellect.

In turn, William E. Sheriff praises the portrayal of Richard for its prodigious fusion of tragedy and comedy: "As the dramatist developed in his handling of the English history play genre, he obviously became more adept at using comic elements to enrich his work. He dared to portray his most wicked king as his most comic king." Rossiter, too, highlights Richard's comedic traits in the context of his theatricality: "Through his prowess as actor and his embodiment of the comic Vice and impish-to-fiendish humor, he offers the false as more attractive than the true (the actor's function), and the ugly and evil as admirable and amusing (the clown's game of value reversals)." Indeed, from almost every imaginable perspective, critics have praised and wondered at the extraordinary, sometimes paradoxical complexity of Shakespeare's King Richard III.

The play *Richard III* is often considered in its context in Shakespeare's First Tetralogy, where it is the closing entry, following the three parts of *Henry VI*. August Wilhelm von Schlegel, quoted by Howard Staunton in *The Complete Illustrated Shakespeare*, asserts that in terms of tone and content, the four do function together as a unified work. Comparing the quality of *Henry VI, Part Three* and *Richard III*, E. M. W. Tillyard gives the latter qualified praise: "In style the play is better sustained than its predecessor. There is less undifferentiated stuff, and the finest pieces of writing (as distinguished from the finest scenes) are more dramatic." Tillyard speaks less enthusiastically about the overall length and pace of the play in light of Shakespeare's artistic endurance, contending, "Richard's plotting with Buckingham and his acquisition of the throne though strongly organized must have tired Shakespeare. There are even signs of strain in the last stage of the process when Richard appears between the two bishops; the verse droops somewhat. After this … the vitality flags, except in patches." Other commentators offer similar criticism of minor or peripheral aspects of the play. Rossiter notes that certain scenes, like the collective lamentation of Queens Margaret and Elizabeth and the Duchess of York, constitute such contrived "quasi-realistic costume-play stuff" that "even editors have found the proceedings absurd." Overall, however, critics have expressed great appreciation for this fairly early Shakespearean history.

What Do I Read Next?

- Christopher Marlowe's *Tamburlaine the Great, Parts I and II* (1590) retells the story of a Mongol warrior who, like Richard, uses deception to rise to power and eventually meets his downfall.

- John Milton's epic poem *Paradise Lost* (1667) features the character of Satan, to whom Shakespeare's Richard has been compared.

- In her novel *The Daughter of Time* (1951), featuring a modern British detective who decides to investigate Richard's crimes, mystery writer Josephine Tey offers a sympathetically revised portrait of Richard III.

- Desmond Seward offers a historical

account of the life of this play's main character in the biographical *Richard III: England's Black Legend* (1982).

Sources

Berman, Ronald, "Anarchy and Order in *Richard III and King John*," in *Shakespeare Survey*, Vol. 20, 1967, pp. 51-9.

Blanpied, John W., "The Dead-End Comedy of *Richard III*," originally published in *Time and the Artist in Shakespeare's English Histories*, Associated University Presses, 1983, pp. 85-97.

Brooks, Harold F., "*Richard III*, Unhistorical Amplifications: The Women's Scenes and Seneca," in *Modern Language Review*, Vol. 75, No. 4, October 1980, pp. 721-37.

Dillon, Janette, "'I Am Myself Alone': *Richard III*," in *Shakespeare and the Solitary Man*, Rowman and Littlefield, 1981, pp. 49-60.

Eccles, Mark, "Introduction," in *The Tragedy of Richard the Third*, by William Shakespeare, edited by Mark Eccles, Signet Classic, 1988, pp. lxiii-lxxi.

——————, "*Richard III* on Stage and Screen," in *The Tragedy of Richard the Third*, by William Shakespeare, edited by Mark Eccles, Signet Classic, 1988, pp. 232-45.

Frisch, Morton J., "Shakespeare's Richard III and the Soul of the Tyrant," originally published in *Interpretation: A Journal of Political Philosophy*, Vol. 20, No. 3, Spring 1993, pp. 275-84.

Gurr, Andrew, "Richard III and the Democratic

Process," in *Essays in Criticism*, Vol. 24, No. 1, January 1974, pp. 39-47.

Heilman, Robert B., "Satiety and Conscience: Aspects of Richard III," in *The Antioch Review*, Vol. 24, No. 1, Spring 1964, pp. 57-73.

Kahn, Coppélia, "'Myself Alone': *Richard III* and the Dissolution of Masculine Identity," in *The Tragedy of Richard the Third*, by William Shakespeare, edited by Mark Eccles, Signet Classic, 1988, pp. 227-31.

Kott, Jan, "The Kings," in *Shakespeare Our Contemporary*, translated by Boleslaw Taborski, Methuen & Co., 1965, pp. 3-46.

Krieger, Murray, "The Dark Generations of *Richard III*," *Criticism*, Vol. 1, No. 1, Winter 1959, pp. 32-48.

Muir, Kenneth, "Image and Symbol in Shakespeare's Histories," in *Bulletin of the John Rylands Library*, Vol. 50, 1967–1968, pp. 103-23.

Neill, Michael, "Shakespeare's Halle of Mirrors: Play, Politics, and Psychology in *Richard III*," in *Shakespeare Studies*, Vol. 8, 1980, pp. 99-129.

Nietzsche, Friedrich, *Beyond Good and Evil: Prelude to a Philosophy of the Future*, translated by Walter Kaufmann, Vintage Books, 1966.

Norwich, John Julius, *Shakespeare's Kings*, Charles Scribner's Sons, 1999.

Ornstein, Robert, "*Richard III*," in *A Kingdom for a Stage: The Achievement of Shakespeare's History*

Plays, Harvard University Press, 1972.

Richards, Jeffrey, "The Riddle of Richard III," in *History Today*, Vol. 33, No. 8, August 1983, pp. 18-25.

Ritchey, David, "Queen Margaret (*Richard III*): A Production Note," in *North Carolina Journal of Speech and Drama*, Vol. 7, No. 2, 1973, pp. 37-41.

Rossiter, A. P., "Angel with Horns: The Unity of *Richard III*," in *Angel with Horns and Other Shakespeare Lectures*, Longmans, 1961, pp. 1-22.

Shakespeare, William, *The Complete Illustrated Shakespeare*, edited by Howard Staunton, 1858, reprint, Park Lane, 1979.

——————, *The Tragedy of Richard the Third*, edited by Mark Eccles, Signet Classic, 1988.

Shaw, George Bernard, *Shaw on Shakespeare*, edited by Edwin Wilson, E. P. Dutton, 1961.

Sheriff, William E., "The Grotesque Comedy of *Richard III*," originally published in *Studies in the Literary Imagination*, Vol. 5, No. 1, April 1972, pp. 51-64.

Tanner, Stephen L., "Richard III versus Elizabeth: An Interpretation," in *Shakespeare Quarterly*, Vol. 24, No. 4, Autumn 1973, pp. 468-72.

Tillyard, E. M. W., "*Richard III*," originally published in *Shakespeare's History Plays*, Chatto & Windus, 1944, pp. 198-214.

Velz, John W., "Episodic Structure in Four Tudor Plays: A Virtue of Necessity," in *Comparative*

Drama, Vol. 6, No. 2, Summer 1972, pp. 87-102.

Weber, Karl, "Shakespeare's *Richard III*, I.iv.24-33," in *Explicator*, Vol. 38, No. 3, Spring 1980, pp. 24-6.

Wilson, John Dover, "Introduction," in *Richard III*, by William Shakespeare, Cambridge University Press, 1954, pp. vii-xlv.

Further Reading

Fields, Bertram, *Royal Blood: Richard III and the Mystery of the Princes*, Regan Books, 2000.

> A lawyer as well as a writer, Fields approaches the historical records from the time of Richard III with a well-honed skepticism and ability to conjecture, offering revisions of the more one-sided versions of the king's story.

Hicks, Michael, *The Wars of the Roses: 1455–1485*, Routledge, 2003.

> Hicks provides a thought-provoking discussion of the causes of the Wars of the Roses in this relatively concise volume.

Marshall, Christopher D., *Beyond Retribution: A New Testament Vision for Justice, Crime, and Punishment*, William B. Eerdmans Publishing Company, 2001.

> This even-keeled work discusses concepts of justice found in the Bible and considers their relevance to modern institutionalized systems of justice.

Olivier, Laurence, *On Acting*, Simon & Schuster, 1987.

Widely recognized as one of the greatest Shakespearean actors in history, Olivier provides a far-reaching discussion on the nature of acting, drawing on the lessons he learned playing the most demanding Shakespearean roles, including that of Richard III.

9 781375 387095